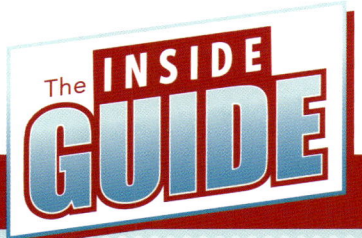

CIVICS

Taxes

By Cassie M. Lawton

New York

Published in 2021 by Cavendish Square Publishing, LLC
243 5th Avenue, Suite 136, New York, NY 10016

Copyright © 2021 by Cavendish Square Publishing, LLC

First Edition

No part of this publication may be reproduced, stored in a retrieval system, or transmitted in any form or by any means—electronic, mechanical, photocopying, recording, or otherwise—without the prior permission of the copyright owner. Request for permission should be addressed to Permissions, Cavendish Square Publishing, 243 5th Avenue, Suite 136, New York, NY 10016. Tel (877) 980-4450; fax (877) 980-4454.

Website: cavendishsq.com

This publication represents the opinions and views of the author based on his or her personal experience, knowledge, and research. The information in this book serves as a general guide only. The author and publisher have used their best efforts in preparing this book and disclaim liability rising directly or indirectly from the use and application of this book.

All websites were available and accurate when this book was sent to press.

Portions of this work were originally authored by Leslie Harper and published as *Why Do We Pay Taxes? (Civics Q&A)*. All new material this edition authored by Cassie M. Lawton.

Library of Congress Cataloging-in-Publication Data

Names: Lawton, Cassie M., author.
Title: Taxes / by Cassie M. Lawton.
Description: First edition. | New York, NY : Cavendish Square Publishing, LLC, 2021. | Series: The inside guide: civics |
Includes bibliographical references and index.
Identifiers: LCCN 2020004866 (print) | LCCN 2020004867 (ebook) |
ISBN 9781502657152 (library binding) | ISBN 9781502657138 (paperback) |
ISBN 9781502657145 (set) | ISBN 9781502657169 (ebook)
Subjects: LCSH: Taxation–United States–Juvenile literature.
Classification: LCC HJ2362 .L39 2021 (print) | LCC HJ2362 (ebook) |
DDC 336.200973–dc23
LC record available at https://lccn.loc.gov/2020004866
LC ebook record available at https://lccn.loc.gov/2020004867

Editor: Kristen Susienka
Copy Editor: Nathan Heidelberger
Designer: Tanya Dellaccio

The photographs in this book are used by permission and through the courtesy of: Cover D. Pimborough/Shutterstock.com; p. 4 kali9/E+/Getty Images; p. 6 antoniodiaz/Shutterstock.com; p. 7 Westend61/Getty Images; p. 8 Hill Street Studios/DigitalVision/Getty Images; p. 9 Joaquin Corbalan P/Shutterstock.com; p. 10 Travelpix Ltd/Stone/Getty Images; p. 12 Thomas Barwick/Stone/Getty Images; p. 13 JHVEPhoto/Shutterstock.com; p. 14 Tupungato/Shutterstock.com; p. 15 Peter Byrne/PA Images/Getty Images; p. 16 Zach Gibson/Getty Images News/Getty Images; p. 18 https://upload.wikimedia.org/wikipedia/commons/6/6c/Constitution_of_the_United_States%2C_page_1.jpg; p. 19 (both) Rob Crandall/Shutterstock.com; p. 20 RichLegg/E+/Getty Images; p. 22 Westend61/Getty Images; p. 24 MediaNews Group/Orange County Register/Getty Images; p. 25 Susan Montgomery/Shutterstock.com; p. 26 Michael Tullberg/Getty Images Entertainment/Getty Images; p. 27 Rido/Shutterstock.com; p. 28 (top left) Matteo Colombo/DigitalVision/Getty Images; p. 28 (top right) Stockr/Shutterstock.com; p. 29 (bottom) Stuart Monk/Shutterstock.com; p. 29 (top left) WDG Photo/Shutterstock.com; p. 29 (top right) Robert Nicholas/OJO/Getty Images; p. 29 (bottom left) Leonard Zhukovsky/Shutterstock.com; p. 29 (bottom right) Tupungato/Shutterstock.com.

CPSIA compliance information: Batch #CS20CSQ: For further information contact Cavendish Square Publishing LLC, New York, New York, at 1-877-980-4450.

Printed in the United States of America

CONTENTS

Chapter One:	5
Taxes: What Are They?	
Chapter Two:	11
Federal, State, and Local Taxes	
Chapter Three:	17
The Government and Taxes	
Chapter Four:	23
Why Taxes Matter	
Key Taxes in America	28
Think About It!	29
Glossary	30
Find Out More	31
Index	32

Taxes help pay for things like public schools and school buses.

TAXES: WHAT ARE THEY?

Chapter One

Libraries, public schools, parks, and roads are important parts of every community. It costs money to put books in libraries and schools and to build parks and roads for a community to use. Where does this money come from? It comes from taxes!

Taxes are money people pay the government. People pay taxes on money they earn and money they spend. The government then uses this money to provide fire stations, post offices, schools, and other important things in a community. Without taxes, our country would be a very different place. Keep reading to learn about how taxes work and what they pay for.

Different Kinds of Taxes

People pay different types of taxes. Some examples of taxes are sales tax, income tax, and property tax. They all help pay for important things in the United States today.

Sales Tax

The next time you're shopping, look at the price of something you plan to buy. When you pay for it, the cost may be higher than what was on the price tag. That extra money you're charged is called a sales tax.

In the United States, sales tax generally isn't put on price tags. It's added to items when you go to pay for them.

The amount that you pay in sales tax is a percentage of what an item costs. That means that if the sales tax in your state is 8 percent, you would pay 8 cents in sales tax for every dollar that you spend. The percentage that's charged for a sales tax is decided by each state. Also, the county or city in which you live may have additional sales tax on top of your state's sales tax.

Fast Fact

Some states have no sales tax. They include Alaska, Delaware, Montana, New Hampshire, and Oregon.

Property Taxes

If your parents own a house, they likely pay a property tax each year. Property is a house or building people own. People who own houses, apartment buildings, or buildings for businesses pay property taxes. City and county governments collect property taxes. A local government uses this money to pay for services the community needs, such as public schools.

To decide how much someone will pay in property taxes, a **tax assessor** must first decide how much a property is worth. This person looks at where the property is located, what improvements have been made to the property, and the value of nearby properties. The property tax owed is a percentage of what the property is worth.

Experts can help people better understand the taxes they pay.

Fast Fact
Some states, such as Florida, don't collect income taxes. However, people who live in these states still pay federal income taxes.

Taxes help pay for police officers in our communities.

Income Taxes

An income tax is a tax people pay based on how much money they earn each year. Generally, the more money people earn, the more income tax they pay. Workplaces usually take the money out of a person's **paycheck** each time they're paid. Then, the federal, or national, government collects this money. Many state and local governments collect their own income taxes as well.

Once a year, people file, or report, their income taxes with the **Internal Revenue Service** (IRS) to make sure they've paid the correct amount. If they've paid too little, they'll owe the government money. If they've paid too much, the government gives them a **refund**.

Fast Fact
If a person's income tax is not taken from their paycheck, they must send income tax payments directly to the IRS.

TAX DAY

April 15 is usually the day by which every American needs to have their income taxes filed. Many people call this day Tax Day because of that. If people live outside the United States, they can get extra time to file their taxes, called an extension. For those cases, Tax Day is in June or October. There have been other Tax Days throughout US history, though. The first Tax Day was March 1. Later, Tax Day became March 15. In 1954, Tax Day became April 15. It's been that day ever since. If Tax Day falls on a weekend or holiday, however, people have a few days longer to file their taxes. This happens every few years.

Tax Day is an important day for many Americans.

Lawmakers, who work in the US Capitol, decide taxes for the United States.

FEDERAL, STATE, AND LOCAL TAXES

Chapter Two

Taxes pay for different needs and services depending on whether they're a federal tax, a state tax, or a local tax. Federal taxes fund things for the whole country. State and local taxes fund things for individual states and communities, respectively.

Federal Taxes

Federal taxes pay for things that keep the entire country safe and running well. The US federal government spends over 60 percent of its money on three important areas. One area is national security. This is the part of the government that keeps all people living in the country safe. It includes the US military. Another area is Social Security, a program that provides money to people who have retired or can't work. The last major area of spending is health care. This tax money goes to programs that provide health care to people who are elderly, disabled, or very poor.

> **Fast Fact**
> Federal taxes pay for Medicare, which provides health care to the elderly and the disabled. Federal taxes also fund Medicaid, which provides health care for the poor.

The taxes Americans pay help provide health care for the elderly.

State Taxes

State governments get much of their money from state income taxes and sales taxes. States then use this money for many of the things that keep their communities running. On average, states spend about 25 percent of their money on public education. This money is given to local governments, which use it to build schools, buy supplies, and pay teachers.

Each state has at least one public college, and many states have more than one.

State taxes also pay for public colleges, universities, and state parks. The money from state taxes is used to build and fix state highways too. In addition, it provides for state police, who patrol roads to keep people from breaking traffic laws.

Fast Fact
The tax money that supports state colleges and universities helps bring down the fees students pay to attend. The cost of attending college is called tuition.

Local Taxes

Local taxes are taxes paid to a city or county government. They're used for things like building, maintaining, and cleaning town parks. Library books are also paid for by local taxes. Like state taxes, local taxes also help pay for public education.

Most of this money comes from property taxes. First, members of the local government decide how much money they'll need to spend in a year. Then, they decide how much property owners must pay in taxes. Property taxes can change every year based on how much money the government needs.

It's easy to see local taxes in action. Local governments use tax money to pay for things that communities need, such as garbage pickup and hospitals. Communities couldn't stay safe and clean without money from local taxes!

Local taxes in Brooklyn, New York, help fund its public library.

VAT: A EUROPEAN TAX

Countries other than the United States have taxes too; however, their systems are a little different. In Europe, many countries have property taxes and income taxes, as well as something called a value-added tax (VAT). This is an additional price placed on items such as food or clothing. It's different from a sales tax because it's paid in different stages over the course of the creation of an item, instead of all at once when the final product is sold. When a farmer buys tomato seeds, for example, a certain percentage is added to the price of the seeds and is paid to the government as part of the VAT. The farmer then adds value to the seeds by growing them into tomatoes. When the farmer sells the tomatoes to a restaurant, more of the VAT is paid to the government. The restaurant then adds value by cooking those tomatoes into a tasty meal. A further share of the VAT is paid when a customer pays the bill for their meal.

Fast Fact

Over 170 countries have VAT as part of their tax systems.

VAT is printed on receipts, such as this one.

Congress has the power to tax US citizens.

THE GOVERNMENT AND TAXES

Chapter Three

Taxes are a part of many areas of life—including the government. They're also very important when it comes to elections. People who are elected to government positions may make promises about taxes. These promises can help them get elected. Lawmakers, especially those in Congress, play a big **role** in raising or lowering taxes.

Taxes in the Federal Government

The federal government is divided into three parts, or branches: legislative, executive, and judicial. All parts deal with taxes. Congress, which makes up the legislative branch, votes on a budget, which is generally created with advice from the president, the head of the executive branch. The budget states what portion of tax money collected will go to certain areas of the government, such as health care or education. The president has the power to approve or reject the budget. The judicial branch can decide if laws that deal with taxes are unconstitutional, or not in line with the US Constitution.

Congress's Job

The US Constitution is a document that explains how the US government works. It was written in 1787. One part of the Constitution talks about the role of Congress in the US government. Members of Congress write and pass laws about many things, including federal taxes. The power to do this was first given in the Constitution.

Congress decides what types of federal taxes people will pay. It also decides how much each tax will be. It can raise or lower taxes each year. Members of Congress have to think carefully about whether to raise or lower taxes. That's because these decisions affect the lives of every person living in the United States.

The beginning of the US Constitution is shown here.

Fast Fact

The first US income tax was collected in 1862 to raise money to help troops fighting in the **American Civil War**. Before income taxes, the federal government got much of its money by taxing goods imported from other countries.

The IRS

The IRS collects all of the federal tax money in the United States. The IRS is part of the executive branch of the government. The executive branch carries out, or executes, the laws. That means it has the right, or power, to collect taxes once those taxes have been approved by Congress. The IRS is an important part of the executive branch. It works to make sure all citizens are paying taxes. It started in 1862 under a different name and continues today.

This is the IRS Building in Washington, DC.

Always a Responsibility?

As written in the US Constitution, Congress has the right to tax the American people. This means all people in America have a responsibility to pay taxes. People should pay taxes to be good members of their community and to help the country function well. However, some people don't take this responsibility seriously. Sometimes, people don't file their taxes, or they put their money elsewhere so it can't be taxed. This is called tax evasion and is a serious crime.

Fast Fact
Taxes also pay for the **salaries** of government leaders, like members of Congress and the president.

Not paying taxes can put you in jail.

THE TAXPAYER BILL OF RIGHTS

Each person who pays taxes also has certain rights. This is called the Taxpayer Bill of Rights. It's modeled after the Bill of Rights, which is the list of the first 10 amendments, or changes, to the US Constitution. It lays out different rights of a taxpayer. The rights are:

1 the right to be informed

2 the right to **quality** service

3 the right to pay no more than the correct amount of tax

4 the right to challenge the IRS's position and be heard

5 the right to **appeal** an IRS decision in an independent **forum**

6 the right to **finality**

7 the right to privacy

8 the right to **confidentiality**

9 the right to retain representation (to have a lawyer)

10 the right to a fair and just tax system

Fast Fact
People may not have to file taxes if they make below a certain amount of money at their jobs.

Cities like San Francisco, California, have high taxes.

WHY TAXES MATTER

Chapter Four

People have different opinions about taxes. Some people don't like paying them. They think it's unfair that people must give money that they've earned to the government. Other people don't mind paying taxes. They believe in the value of the services their tax money pays for, including programs that help others and the country as a whole. However, even if people don't mind paying taxes, they might not like how high taxes sometimes are. Since the amount of taxes differs according to each community and each person's salary, some people are paying very high taxes. Taxes may be tough to figure out and form an opinion on, but they are beneficial for much of society!

Helping the Military

Taxes help pay for the military. In America, there are thousands of servicemen and women helping keep the country safe. They work inside the United States as well as around the world. Taxes go toward paying them as well as paying for the equipment they use.

Taxes help pay for military uniforms.

After someone leaves military service or retires from the military, they're called a veteran. Taxes help pay for special hospitals, run by the Department of Veterans Affairs (VA), for when a veteran is in need of medical care. They give veterans access to key medical professionals. These hospitals also help veterans deal with the **trauma** that members of the military sometimes experience.

Fast Fact
VA facilities serve over 9 million veterans each year.

Veterans can go to VA hospitals to receive care.

Helping Those in Need

Taxes also help many other Americans. Taxes fund a benefits program called the Supplemental Nutrition Assistance Program (SNAP) that helps **low-income** families buy **nutritious** food. People who benefit from this program get a certain amount of money each month on an **electronic benefits transfer** (EBT) card to pay for their food items. This way, taxes help families in need get food they couldn't get otherwise. SNAP benefits are often referred to as "food stamps."

Taxes also help pay for health care and school lunch programs. Schools provide low-income kids with lunch if they don't bring their own. Taxes pay for these lunches for kids who can't afford them. Programs called Medicare, Medicaid, and the Children's Health Insurance Program (CHIP) also help families afford health insurance. CHIP works closely with Medicaid, but it's for families who make enough money that they can't sign on to Medicaid. Each program benefits people every day.

Fast Fact
Each state has its own SNAP program to help those in need, though the money comes from the federal government.

What Can You Do?

While you're too young to have to worry about income tax or property

25

AFFORDING HEALTH CARE

Some politicians have big hopes for the future of taxes. One hot topic is universal health care, or free health services for all. Some politicians hope that taxes can one day make this possible. The ideal setup, according to politicians like Bernie Sanders, is Medicare for All. This would allow key programs and health services to be accessible for all people living in the United States. It would use tax money to fund services like doctor and hospital visits, surgeries, and other medical care for everyone.

One example of the movement toward universal health care is the Affordable Care Act (ACA). Passed in 2010, the ACA expanded Medicaid and provided money to help people buy health insurance. In the United States, if you don't have health insurance, you might have to pay a lot for visits to the doctor and hospitals. Not everybody likes the idea of universal health care, however, because taxes would likely increase a lot to make it possible.

Senator Bernie Sanders of Vermont is a big supporter of Medicare for All.

tax, you can do things in your community to be more aware about taxes. For example, the next time you go to the store, you can look at your receipt. On it, you'll see the total amount spent on your items. Underneath that, you'll probably see an added sales tax line, followed by the complete total for the purchase.

To learn more about taxes, you can ask your parents or a guardian about their filing process. You can also visit the websites of the IRS, Congress, and your state and local governments to find out how taxes are used at the federal, state, and local levels.

By being more aware of taxes in your community and the nation, you can best prepare for your future as a taxpayer.

Fast Fact
Businesses also have to pay taxes. The taxes they pay to the government are called corporate income taxes.

Taxes Help Everyone

In the end, everyone benefits from at least some of the things taxes pay for. Taxes help keep our communities running smoothly and safely. Even though not everyone will use every service that taxes pay for, we can think of these services as safety nets. If we ever need them, they'll be there!

With an adult's permission, you can learn more about taxes by searching online.

KEY TAXES IN AMERICA

Below you can find key taxes in the United States today; whether they're state, local, or federal; and which parts of a community they help.

property tax
local
libraries, sewer/water systems, schools, city parks

sales tax
state/local
state parks, building projects, roads, teachers, police

income tax
federal/state/local
military, education, Social Security, health care

THINK ABOUT IT!

1. What do you think are some of the most important things taxes pay for in a community?

2. Why is it important to pay taxes? What would happen if there weren't any taxes?

3. Think about how taxes are used. What are some new areas taxes could be used for to help a community?

4. Why might some people be upset about paying taxes? Do you think lowering taxes is something government leaders should try to do?

GLOSSARY

American Civil War: A war that took place from 1861 to 1865 between the North (Union) and the South (Confederacy) in the United States.

appeal: To ask for another review of a matter or situation.

confidentiality: An understanding to not make matters public.

electronic benefits transfer: A system that gives low-income families money each month through cards, which are used much like credit cards or debit cards to purchase items.

finality: An end.

forum: A place for discussions about a topic.

Internal Revenue Service: The part of the US government that collects federal taxes.

low-income: Earning little money through work.

nutritious: Healthy; full of nutrients and vitamins.

paycheck: An amount of money received from a job in a certain time period that often comes in the form of a check.

quality: Good or in good condition.

refund: Money given back to a person.

role: A part or job.

salary: A set amount of money a person makes at a job per year, not based on the amount of hours they work.

tax assessor: A person who decides how much a property is worth.

trauma: A bad or frightening thing that happened to someone.

FIND OUT MORE

Books

Andal, Walter. *Finance 101 for Kids: Money Lessons Children Cannot Afford to Miss*. Minneapolis, MN: Mill City Press, 2016.

McGillan, Jamie Kyle. *The Kids' Money Book*. New York, NY: Sterling Children's Books, 2016.

Small, Cathleen. *How Does Congress Work?* New York, NY: Lucent Press, 2019.

Websites

IRS
www.irs.gov
This is the official website of the IRS.

United States Taxes
www.usa.gov/taxes
This website explains the tax system in the United States, as well as provides information about filing taxes and tax returns.

Why Do We Need Taxes?
www.ducksters.com/history/us_government/taxes.php
This website explores taxes, why we need them, what they do, and how they work.

Publisher's note to educators and parents: Our editors have carefully reviewed these websites to ensure that they are suitable for students. Many websites change frequently, however, and we cannot guarantee that a site's future contents will continue to meet our high standards of quality and educational value. Be advised that students should be closely supervised whenever they access the Internet.

INDEX

A
American Civil War, 18

B
budget, 17

C
Children's Health Insurance Program (CHIP), 25
Congress, 10, 16, 17, 18, 19, 20, 27
Constitution, US, 17, 18, 20, 21
corporate income tax, 27

E
education, 4, 5, 7, 12–13, 17
extension, 9

F
federal government, 8, 10, 11, 16, 17–20, 21, 23–25, 26, 27
filing taxes, 8, 9, 20, 21, 27

H
health care, 11, 12, 14, 17, 24, 25, 26

I
imports, 18
income tax, 5, 8, 9, 12, 15, 18, 25–27
Internal Revenue Service (IRS), 8, 19, 21, 27

L
libraries, 5, 13, 14
local government, 6, 7, 8, 11, 12, 13–14, 27

M
Medicaid, 11, 25, 26
Medicare, 11, 25, 26
military, 11, 23–24

P
parks, 5, 13
police, 8, 13
president, 17, 20
property tax, 5, 7, 8, 13, 15, 25–27

R
refund, 8
responsibility, 20
roads, 5, 13

S
sales tax, 5–6, 12, 15, 27
school lunches, 25
Social Security, 11
state government, 6, 8, 11, 12–13, 23, 25, 27
Supplemental Nutrition Assistance Program (SNAP), 25

T
tax assessor, 7
Tax Day, 9
tax evasion, 20
Taxpayer Bill of Rights, 21

V
value-added tax (VAT), 15
veterans, 24, 25